Presence & Its Shadow

Written by
Michael Angel Loayza Jr.

The Opening

Love knows no time.

Nothing blinds and minds the heart other than the mind and its intentions.

Heartache stems from the identification with the mind and its form – once one becomes aware of this fear no longer binds the heart.

Suffering becomes Enlightenment. Ego becomes Presence. Dark becomes Light. Birth is painful yet leads to beauty – who is to say that Death is not the same?

Just as Enlightenment has its counterpart Suffering, Presence has its shadow that they call Ego.

I now sing to you from prison while being innately at peace.

$\mathfrak{I}$ would like to begin by letting you know that some of these poems are written with the exploitative use of the ego and some are simply of a higher consciousness – though when expelled egoically they are still being observed (by the experiencer) through the eyeless eyes of presence. Some of the poems to follow begin as observations and articulations of the ego and then naturally molt into a higher source of being. I'll let the reader decide which is which. I am aware that I am not these attached, possessive and materialistic thoughts, but I feel that shameless exploitation is a healthy way to reflect and disidentify with thoughts and emotions that attempt to run us out of our innate way of being; it brings the formless taunts that are at times whispered and screamed by the ego into form and exploits it for what it is: a warped perception of the fragmented and fictitious reality within our minds rather than the external reality in which we observe and that is beyond our mind and conceptualization – the space between the thoughts and between each breath brings us back home – it brings is back to what *is* and even what is not.

Reality simply just is. Reality also is not. Overall, I wish that this grounds you into the present moment and time falls away along with superficiality and something greater then occurs – something that I cannot truly articulate by words or thought.

We are all mirrors of one and other. We are even able to see a world within a world within the eye of a Present Other – that is how powerful this unity with the Present moment is. The ego will ask "Is this all?" but great innate faith truly knows what *is* and too paradoxically "knows" nothing at all.

Rooted in this moment all becomes peace even when peace is seemingly lost. This is God. This is Nature. This is the Universe. And I shall no longer spoil it or devalue it with the mind's articulation. But I will humbly exploit all sides of reality through the poetry that is soon to follow these flowing words.

As I write to candlelight and listen to the gentle kisses of rain, I wish you peace, love, kindness, and innate presence.

Lightning has just struck. A star has fallen. A new star is born – or may it just be the very same star in a different form?

Oyster

Your life is what it is –

Moments go by,
Memories are missed –

If I could heal the world
Of all of its pain,
I would sacrifice myself,
I would give my only name –

I write from this place
As I heal the world –

Find yourself;
Find your pearl.

Free Spirit

I love you girl
Can't you see,
But the artist is to be forever free;

You cannot chain him,
Leave him alone,
Stop trying to take him from his home –

If you accept this then you two will forever be,
Don't let your love drown in the sea.

Laughter

Children laughing & playing
To the sunset on a cool blanket of snow –
This is it for all who knows.

Mood

She undresses in front of me;
Her curves guide my eyes to heaven –

She then asks what am I thinking;

I say nothing,
I just think to myself
That it's you that I'm drinking –

I long for your touch,
To feel your clenching warm embrace –

My soul slides into yours as two become one –

I see it in your eyes,
I see the rising sun.

See

White spotted trees,
The clouds moving fast,
All is so beautiful,
All is so glass –

Clear blue skies and
Cotton-white clouds
Sit behind quickly moving grey clouds:
Patience.

Above

The sky's beauty
Never gets old,
It heals my body;
It heals my soul.

Her

Watching the master play,
A smile fills my face;
If only I could hold her –
If only I can taste...

I feel the world dancing
Around me
As I dance within;
I feel the universe calling
As I continue to work
To win –

All is beautiful,
All tastes so good –
My thoughts are nothing:
All is good.

Once Upon A Time

I once used to fear going to sleep,
I once use to fear waking up;

I'm now guided by the stars,
I no longer exist –

I am one with the Universe,
I am one with the Earth's mist.

Falling

Life breathes amidst
The dead fallen leaves,

Flowers bloom and sing
To the bees –

Nature's beauty...
Again, on my knees.

Who

Free spirit,
Loving soul,
Within our friendship
I am whole –

A snowflake in solitude;

Unity:

A blanket exudes
And lightens the mood.

Rain

The rain falls and all is
Vibrant green
With the smell of the trees –

The beauty of death
Amongst the foliage is that
There is nothing left;

No leaves or trees
Or a reason to be wept.

Room

The reflection is so beautiful;
Raindrops,
A young girl with a rose,
Glowing salt...

It's not her fault
She doesn't see it;
It's not her fault
She cannot be it –
But it is her choice
To smother her
One and only voice –

Rooted in what is,
In this is tranquil breath
Is bliss;
Live, laugh, love,
Heaven is here,
Not up above.

Bones II

My mind is now free,
My soul sheds a tear,
I worry no more,
I swear the end was clear
And life was all I could hear –

My bones are one with the dirt,
Rooted in the fire,
The storm has burnt out
All of my past desires.

Guided by the warm sun,
A smile on my face;
An impromptu laugh –
All is in bloom,
Too my soul
And the taste.

Losing Game

Love doesn't compare,
Love doesn't contrast,
Love doesn't even truly last –
Caught in illusions
As your body remains tense,
You're in a battle with something
That you cannot win against.

Waiting

I long for you to return home
I long you for to know that you're not alone -
I long for you to find yourself
While I sit in the center
And I cannot help;

You're missing and not living,
You disappeared,
You were eaten away by your deepest fears –

You attempt to destroy all the love you receive
Based on a story told
In a time of need -
Actions speak louder than words -
Stars shine higher than the wings of birds –

Wake up, it's okay to cry -
Wake up, don't kiss life goodbye...
You have people that love you,
It's you that tells yourself you're alone –

It's you that pushes everyone away
To make it on your own -
Presence always pervades the darkest cloud but you
Choose to smother your vibrant light –

This is simply a reminder
That it is within your might.

Beauty

The torturous future and the poisonous past -
Oh, how time makes me laugh.

Let my words sink into your tethered soul
And you'll again soon become whole.

The blinding sun reflecting on the glistening river,
Those who hear it will never be bitter –

Shards of ice floating by with hungry feathered
Ducks diving and floating –

Nature loves us.

Love (a song)

Love will win – won't you let it my friend?
Love will win – won't you let it my friend?
Love will win – won't you let it my friend?

I sit by as I watch you die,
Waiting for your return –
The sky is black but I got your back,
The sun again will burn...

Life may have you beat
And knock you off your feet,
We all will have our turn –
Just let it be and you will see
And within this you will learn...

Love will win – won't you let it my friend?
Love will win – won't you let it my friend?
Love will win – won't you let it my friend?

The clouds have passed,
And these memories last,
But we all must take our turn –
Free yourself, there's nobody else,
Let the fire burn.

Love will win – won't you let it my friend?
Love will win – won't you let it my friend?
Love will win – won't you let it my friend?

Our pain is shared,
We're beyond repair,
But our love can still burn –
There's a hole in the sky
Where we go to die,

The Present's where we live and learn –

But our love will still forever burn.

Tired

Tireless you are,
In your mind you are far;
No better place for you to exist:
The moonlight hue
Upon the ocean mist –

Rippling stars,
Something is right;
I love you, dear,
With all of my might –

Mountaintops high in the sky,
Beneath them opens up with fire
Where the earth meets the eye;
Laying on the frozen water
And looking to the passing clouds –
A crescent moon for two
Screams forever loud.

Healing

My love,
I'm healed –
My love,
I'm too real –
Life is good
And so is your beauty;
Let me exploit it,
For this is my duty:

The sun shines burnt-orange light;
All that is beautiful,
The grass stands tall,
How can one ever fall –

A warm smile and greeting
Lights what eternally is
As the leaves live and fall
To eternal bliss.

God

Father, I love you –
All I want is for us to be together –

The beauty,
The duty,
To go on and freely live:

The moment we love ourselves
And innately choose to give.

Cry

With tears on my pillow
I venture to sleep,
Only to dream what
Will too make me weep –
Illusions and resistances;
This moment,
This day,
Beauty has had
It's final stay.

Pieces of The Sky

A puzzle that fits;
I await you like the sun
Awaits the kiss of the moon,
I await you like the flowers
That are too soon to bloom –

Winter passes,
Time decays,
All moves,
All stays;

"I love you,
I am here" echoes the moon,
"I love you,
I'm always near" as the flowers move to bloom;

We are beyond 'mine' and 'mind' whether
We know it or not –
Without possession
All is truly bought.

Soldier

You are strong,
I'm never wrong,
I'll live with you all nightmare long –
A pit within my gut and the moments it arises;
Love conquers all and together
We mustn't disguise it.

Overcome

I fear nothing,
Not even death itself,
Only you can attain this –
Nobody else.

Deadhead

I follow the moon
As it makes my insides dance,
I'm pulled by the hue,
It has me in a trance.

Elation comes as thoughts leave;
Extremities tingle with the sound of the bees.

An ocean of grey above my head,
The trees dance while I write from bed –
"All is perfect" the wind howls;
My ego then chatters
But I no longer scowl.

Pumpkin

Pumpkin in the sky
And its light is scared to die;
Remember the iris of its eye –

Numbness, I feel –
This is all too real.

I feel nothing,
Tall dancing trees,
Bright green moss,
A flickering stare –
What is its cost?

Growing from the sun
Shining through the window –
The sky pours while trees dance to the wind's blow.

The sun turns into the moon,
A seed eventually blossoms and blooms.

Now halfway in the sky
Lies an erased moon –
A bright star flickers
And its audience swoons.

Love

Warm sun on my skin,
The birds chirp;
My sentient friends…

All is still,
All is quiet –
Look around you –
You can't deny it.

Lion

Caring for you has been the most
Beautiful soul-bounding venture –

This month has solidified a 14-year bond –
I attempted to heal you but nature took its course,
Thus leaving a hole in my heart –

I have become more human –
I have become more of an
Artist than I ever could have –
You have led me to follow my heart and soul –
I love you –

The beauty of loving and healing –
Giving so much of yourself is so
Rewarding to the soul
Yet so painful to the ego –

My life became you through the long month of
February and I'd never have it any other way –
I love you so much;
Your fuzzy smiling face has been my favorite sight
Since you were born –

I'm so grateful for our memories –
How do we live without the ones we love?
The truth is: we don't.
Heaven on earth once existed in your smile,
Now it exists within our
Unchained thoughts of paradise...

Surely heaven is a state of being:
Absent of mind and devoid of time.

War

You look into the eyes of another
And mistake them for your enemy;
They are a mirror of you and yourself –
Do not mistake them for anyone else;

War's value is one thing:
Money is all the missiles sing –
Millions of humans fighting for one insane man
When all can be stopped
With the joining of hands –

War was birthed out of 'want' and 'need' –
It is all for power and endless greed;
The media will tell you how to feel
And what to believe,
But don't let their proprietors foolishly deceive;

The blood is too equally on their hands
As well as this country
And any blind allegiance to man –

Free thought cannot be bought;
We as humans must be taught:

Obedience is death,
Or else all is lost.

We Are Nature

If I don't cry when I sit with my thoughts
Then the sky does –
What happens when the sky cries?
The earth grows –
What happens when there's a drought?
All things suffer –

Crying, like the rain,
Births new life and sustains a healthy ecosystem;
Harboring, like a drought,
Perpetuates death and an unhealthy *ego*-system –
Living in the present accepts all and rejects nothing;
There is kindness and wisdom in this –

One may disagree but I ask you
Where do your stories take you?
To the past or to the future or to both?
Where does your suffering come from?
Your situation? – or what you tell yourself about it?
Who feels this way?
Outside of your breath what truly exists?
Outside of this moment what truly exists?

Reality attempts to tell us what we think it is
But without thought there is only true reality –
This moment is all that exists;
There are no problems to be solved or fixed,
There is only now;
In the Death of Time
Purpose comes forth without effort,
Without planning, without intentions,
All flows naturally like a gently flowing stream –
As the ego dies something profound occurs:
Life itself is birthed,

Or at least that's how it seems.

Tethered

I let myself feel your pain today
Despite the hurt, bitterness, and abuse
I've witnessed –
I saw you as a human.

You chose to cut yourself off,
You chose to become nihilistic without knowing;
We take our anger out on those we love
But you went endlessly and chose to harden –

You shunned your feelings.
I want you to know that despite the pain,
Despite the means to accept reality as it is
Or even as it is not,
We all still love you.

Tension may run high
But it is okay –
The world does not revolve around us and
Despite what you think,
It is the family that has always revolved around you.

We've been there up till the very end.
Looking to the sky through a telescope –
I'll always remember...

There is no shame or embarrassment;
There is only love.
Even when there is not.

Stillness of Truth

There's a stillness within us,
A moment of perpetual patience;
In the moments when the grass is too tall to see
And we search for the light to set us free,
We must remember that we're too
Resilient and strong
And that we can survive
The winds all nightmare long –

We will get pricked and bleed upon the floor,
We will feast upon rebirth and hunger for more –
We will bloom and shed our petals to the wind,
We will die and decay again and again –
Be patient, my friend –
There is no beginning nor is there an end.
We water the soil with our tears and
Plant the seeds of hurt –

We die and decay and bleed into the dirt;

To live is to suffer
And to suffer is to live;
Along this blissful journey
We must give and give and give.

Grandma

I held her hand until it regained its warmth;
I watered her with all of my tears
But her breath wouldn't seem to grow –
It was then that I realized that
My eyes were limited...

The world is quiet and still;
It's as if all has stopped –
Peace euphorically showers me
In a cloak of tingling atoms:
Death now fears me.

Warmth

And though the blanket is warm,
Beneath it is a shivering body
On the brink of a slowly petrified rigor mortis –

Shards of ice create a conclave around
What the body once was:
A vibrant host of infinite light –

Now it lies frozen but still warm,
Patiently waiting to die.

That Kind of Love

The perfect kind of love –
As the sun dies and blue hour is in full bloom,
Lit only by the glow of the lightening bugs and
The hungry moon that is covered by a grey blanket,
I embrace my solitude to the fullest –

Within this beauty and beyond the void of loneliness,
I choose Presence –
There is this perfect kind of love that
I've observed throughout my life;
A love that is joined so strongly yet
They don't share the same bed –

It is a beautiful bond that cannot be broken –
It is so strong that it permeates to all –

Can you love someone without touching them?
Can you handle not kissing them for eternity?

A love so strong that it can't be tainted by "love" –
What truly is of its essence?

God.

Nano

It's here.
I look to the tall trees amidst the crystal-clear sky –
In this moment a smile takes my face
Because I have it all yet I have nothing –
In this contains an ounce of something.

The Look

Her face,
The way she looks at me,
With her passion, admiration, appreciation;

Her smile is genuine and without malice –
Her voice is of an angel and her mind is vast
And lights up my own –

A compassionate mother but beyond this is the
Playful inquisitiveness of a child;
She's rare and I'm grateful to know her –
A best friend is birthed through the
Gentle reminder of one and other's worth –

A euphoric connection makes it that much "better" –
It speaks louder than words and
Connects us to what we cannot see –
So just be present and
Let things be.

The Fade

When worth becomes one-sided
And the unconditional love becomes misguided,
Know that the ego has sneakily taken its course;

This is a recipe for misery,
This is a recipe for divorce –

A best friend is now lost
At this superficially-material cost.

The Night

Her body was warm,
It was so long since I've felt another
Warm body against mine –

Her smile said it all,
The happiness, the presence, all free from all of that
Had once ailed her –

I was too free from what ailed me –
In just moments we healed each other,
Just in the simplicity of our shared warm embrace –

It was her smile upon my waking
That told me all that I needed to know –
Which was nothing...

It was unworldly and unearthly –
This made me happy;
It makes me happy –

To share myself with someone that truly deserves it;
To share myself with someone
That is wholesomely worth it.

Egoless

Hills of grass and singing chimes,
Our love was once blossomed and so divine;
Now you choose to live and die
While I stand here breathing
As tears subside –

Push and pull,
I can no longer stay;
You've lost yourself
And do not want to find your way –

I cannot tell you how to live,
This is within your own choice,
But I cannot swallow my pain
When I have this free and singing voice –

Don't throw familiar pieces of you away
Just because your ego wants to play;
Yesterday was a sunny day
And now all is dark and seems decayed –

If you let yourself be then you will see,
Again, you'll blossom
And be forever free –

The more walls you build the further you descend,
You then make a decision
Where you choose to no longer mend,

You eventually become what
You've always desired to be:
The listener of your story and alone in the sea –

I sit at the center of the circle and contemplate
The return for all sentient beings,
I breathe out love and kindness with these words
That contain all seeing.

The Gift of The Stars

The young man exits and looks to the vibrant stars
Shining in the sky –
Tears fill his eyes –

Millions of miles away exists a mirroring
Beauty of our own reflection;

But the midnight hour is blinded by
Our ignorant light and planned intentions –

The stars attempt to guide us back to our
Innate sense of purpose while repeatedly being
Forgotten about due to man's ability
To create artificial light.

Blinded by all that exudes uniqueness,
The world eventually ate itself,
And then regurgitated a new life,
With a new purpose
That was intended to not be eschewed.

Snowfall

Soft snow kisses –
My body is free,
My soul is lifted –

I'm empty
And how beautiful –

I love you,
Smiling trees
Breathing in the fresh air –

A beautiful life,
A sacred moment
Without a care –

A cool blue hue;
Freedom with nothing to do.

Staring

Looking out the window;
Stillness –

Grey skies,
Tall trees,
Two doves,
Weakened knees –

Loving emptiness,
Heavy eyes,
No resistance
To all that dies –

Time is gone
And all who isn't –

Encased in ice,
The frigid water pulses
And travels down the limbs of the tree
Like pulsing veins –

Empowered by the sight
By body lets me be –

Patience, it cries:
We never ever truly die
And now I see.

Mom

Sitting,
Smiling,
Listening to music
And sharing words,

My body then levitates
And flies with the birds –

Nothing more,
Nothing less –

My mother's smile,
My mirrored best.

Shadow

The angel's silhouette
Amidst the fiery forest,
The coupled mourning doves
Humming my favorite chorus,

The roses seek the sun to grow;
Time then fades to all that know –

I'm here,
Which is nowhere to be found –

No longer lost in thought,
My ego has drowned.

Woman In The Street

She punishes herself for her burden-laced life –
She's lost in her thoughts
And doesn't know wrong from right –

She pushes away
All that is uplifting
Because she wants to drown –

And when she smiles
She tells herself that she frowns.

Love

The sight above,
The sight below,

The hugging breath
And
All the grows –

We once were the perfect pieces
To our puzzle –

And now we look to one and other
Muzzled.

Beauty

The sun sets behind the tall trees;
A glowing ball that floats with ease –

Hello moon,
I'll see you soon –

The birds singing,
The soft grass,
The warm sun,
The cool wind –

Nature is the forever friend.

Fading

Love yourself before anyone else;
Let the stairs guide you
Back to yourself –

All becomes one,
All becomes none.

Longing

I could still love you
If you let me –

But you punish yourself
So now we wept thee.

Inca

Cruising with my protector,
The sky is pink, blue and grey –
A crescent moon guides my way –

How beautiful,
And in it I stay –

I fear nothing,
I adore you,
I love and forever endure truth –

Cool earthing mist,
A grounding breath,
Swaying trees;
Nothing's left –

Beauty right outside of my window;
Silhouettes give themselves to the wind's blow –

They become one with the misty dew;
And all who miss it,
Their lives are through.

Empty

I'm empty,
Chatter speaks
But it doesn't call me –

Me is gone –

I care about no time and nothing –

I smile stupidly
And stare to the dancing midnight trees –

What is this...

I feel like not doing anything else –

All is truly good.

Massive

The sun falls to the sky's cliff
And glows –

The beauty of its view is for all who knows –

The night sky had such a strong vibrancy,
It pulled a smile from my face –

My stars were pulsing,
The clouds were coasting –

I became a piece of the painting –

Dancing trees,
Weak knees –

Snow falls,
Here comes the bees.

Bitter

Keep pushing me away
And I'll no longer stay;

I don't want this toxicity
Or the angst it gives to me.

Skies

Cold gentle kisses,
Cotton gracefully falling from the sky,
What beauty in the silence
When the winter clouds cry –

All of its beauty fell into the earth
After being kissed by the sun –

All then became eternally numb –

The breath –
Nothing left –

Time goes by and
The stars I've wept.

Warmth

Sitting in warmth
As the sun warms our soul,

Nature again let's all become whole –

In your eyes I see myself –

Your beauty's truth and nothing else.

Mystery

The energy that flows through me
Flows through you –

I awoke with electric energy throughout my body –

The glow of the moon makes my heart swoon –

Tall hills,
The sound of nature,
All is beautiful,
All is the savior –

How I love you,
Happy and free –

Lightning strikes
And the silhouettes of mountains
Are encased within the sky –

Here I am –
I have died.

Partner

I watch her sleep,
My body warm,

Wishing that I was with her –
Thinking about yesterday
When time was no longer bitter...

A reflection where the sun goes to die –
Where some move on
And where other men try –

Empty like night,
Full like the sun,
But here I am –
I shall no longer run.

Dionysus

Laughter and wine
Where the sky is sublime –

Day becomes night
And mountainous silhouettes flash
With each bolt of lightning –

Trees fall all around me
But none of this is frightening –

The gentle rain falls outside of my window,
My breath sounds like the gentle wind's blow –

I am empty
Despite my body being full with vigor –

With each breath my heart grows bigger.

Nerves

Tingling throughout my body,
A smile upon my face,
My furry friends kissing me,
Playing for endless days –

I am at a moment at a time
That supposedly does not exist –

It's so pure and real;
This is surely endless bliss –

How many times can I write the same thing? –
But what is inarticulate
I shall attempt to sing.

Fearless

As each breath brings me closer to death,
I stand and look to the starry skies –

It's within your glimmer
That I've truly died –

I see right down to your soul
And crave your warm embrace –

I miss the way you smell,
I miss the way you taste.

Mountainous Clouds

I find my way,
All the seasons pass through the day –

The sun shines,
The clouds part,
Rain falls
And all is dark –

Ice falls from the sky,
The sun again comes
And all is dry –

We are one with Nature,
Look how the seasons
Pass in a day –

Feel how Time then fades away.

Pines

The children laugh and play
While the pines gently sway –

Moving to the ocean as all is sound,
The cold wind moves
And the frozen ground.

Tension

My jaw attempts to hold onto all that has pained it,
Reflecting on death and the moments that veined it –

Anger is no longer I;
Sadness is its friend but I no longer die –

Once an emotion turned inside out,
I no longer choose to scream and shout –

Productive action marks its way,
In this purgatory I no longer stay –

I sit,
I face it,
And then I play –

Mark my words,
You too will find your way –

My state of mind is beyond reason
And my Higher Self is one with seasons –
Though my heart occasionally aches
Like a star about to combust,
I no longer desire passion,
I no longer desire lust –

I embrace all that comes,
I no longer run –
I am the falling moon,
I am the rising sun –

I am the whole Universe,
I am too God,
I am too incredibly odd –

I am too you,
I am the sky molting
From black to blue.

I am thoughtless and contain all meaning,
I am the reason why this world is gleaming –

I am no better than you –
You are no better than me –
Despite what we've done,
We are forever one with the sea –

Let yourself go and you will forever be free –
The mirror will become clearer
When what's inside becomes superior.

Tension II

When the body is in tune with the present
Thought becomes obsolete –

I feel the waves of sun kissing my hungry feet –

Step gently to the cool earth as the wind blows and
Whistles between the brim of my hat –

Fill up with air and lose care,
Have the patience of a cat.

Desire

I look into your eyes and distract myself with all of
My own fears,

Distancing myself from the heavy heartache I feel;

Angels sing into my ears telling me
That it will be okay;

"Survive, create yourself and live
Another day" they say;

If I could have you then I would kiss you but
I instead strum my strings encased in glass,

Fragile and with each strum I make this
Endless moment last –

The pain is so heavy that I do everything
I can to fight it;

My eye twitches to hold back tears because now
I'm again faced with my deepest fears
And everything despite it –

I choose to not run away,

I choose to live another day,

I choose to better understand and grow –

I choose to never truly know –

I don't fear you but I hear you –

All will be okay –

All will know…

Within the words 'I love you'

Let the flower grow.

Pain Body & Self-Talk

It comes like a storm,
A wave of emotions flowing through my mind;
All turns upside down –

Presence feels trapped to the
Overwhelming rush of emotions –

Pain masks itself in the form of fear –
I leave and go there and to everywhere –

The angst and pain arise from nowhere and
Doesn't truly exist unless I give it energy –

The energy is then wasted and could rather
Be used productively –

I'm aware and always have been aware...
So, it is I that is in power –

There is nothing to fear –

All is okay –

There is no reason to feel down on yourself
After all you've accomplished,

There isn't a reason to create these stories
To make yourself suffer;

There is no reason to be worried about life or death,
Sickness or what's to be –

Living is effortless and without thought –
Never make decisions when you're uncomfortable –

All passes;
Emotions are seasons.

Hearts

Hearts tear apart as the day becomes the dark –

In the night I find my way
While my solitude has had its stay –

Nestled by the warm hug of the universe
I am yours –

The view outside of my window
Is as beautiful as what lies within me
Said the wind's blow.

Primitive

As we sleep
Our hearts become pulsing stars,
Eternal light soon too becomes dark.

Placenta

We're connected;
The same minds,
The same thoughts;

The same beauty,
The same wants –

I love you as you love me;

You birthed me,
We are the sea.

Birth

Birth contains great suffering and
Sometimes too death,

As petals fall, we see what's bare and left –

Crying in and crying out,
This is what life's all about –

Listen to the waves and see passed the tears,
It is within the illusion
That you overcome your fears –

The ocean is God,
The healer of all healers.

Rooted

The trees root into spring midnight air
And is fed by the hue of the moon –

Two love birds across the way hug under moonlight
And enjoy their stay –

They don't want to say goodbye –
Their smile says it all;

The heart forever beckons our call.

Reflection

The smell is infectious as petals gracefully
Fall in awe of the wind's gentle kiss;

The mind comes and goes as there is temporal bliss.

Accept all and you will never fall –
Within the present you will forever stand tall.

Guidance

I walked alongside her
As if she was fading away –

I embraced every sense of life
Pulsing through my veins –

I etched this memory to live eternally
Within my soul –

I love you,
I believe in you,
And forever we will be –

We are one with the moon,
We are one with the sea.

Knowledge

The great beauty
In which I have learned:

Embrace the present and
The body's light;

Observe yourself with all of your might –

The mind is then empty;

A smile fills me and
Nothing tempts me.

Fame

The greats persist,
The greats exist –

With my body aching
And my eyes puffy from tears,

I rebirth with Nature
And conquer my fears –

My aching body and twitch of the eye,

When I awake from sleep

I'll truly thrive.

Chants

My mind and body
Are healthy and free,
My mind and body
Are one with the sea.

Love is key,
For you and for me –
Open your heart and
Set yourself free.

Blooming flowers in the fragrant hour –
I hold bliss in my heart
And light after dark.

Ego

Too much,
Not enough;
A little,
Not enough –

I hold bliss in my heart
And light after dark –

Time melts into one
As hours dwindle and become the sun –

I'm here with nowhere to go
And nothing to do –

I'm here when the sky turns black
And the sun turns blue.

Feeling

The warm sun heals all;
The throat is tight as I attempt to swallow
These old childish thoughts
That are dead and hollow –

What ails me? – nothing
What pains me? – something

It's okay to simply just heal –
This will too pass –
Just simply feel.

Tightness in the throat
As it becomes hard to swallow,
These thoughts are on repeat;

They are empty and hollow –
Through growth comes old stories of the past –

Nothing that is relevant,
Nothing that can last.

Even when there is a weight upon my chest,
I will not run,
I am at my best.

Release

What peace I've found in dying,
I am now one
And the music is even more beautiful than before –

Let the ego die by accepting what it is
And what is not –

Life will then shine
And the lesson will be taught.

Peace cannot be found,
Nor can it be bought.

Peace simply just is –
It cannot even truly be taught.

Lessons

Dew drops down the stalk of grass
In the tiny village –

The sweet smell of the forest
As it heals my soul.

The Elder

All that you've lived through
And here you are –

It's been a pleasure to know you
And even more so to show you.

Discipline

Tame the mind by doing the work,
Take off your shoes and walk in the dirt.

How simple the joy of seeing you is –
How grateful I am –

These moments of bliss.

Egos

Do I long for you or your company? –
I fear your toxic vice –

I'm waiting for a kiss
That is beyond wrong or right.

Daylight

Love comes and love goes –
It forever stays for the one
That knows...

Heartache comes with the rain
As the flowers begin to bloom;
We cry our eyes all day
While our heart beats to the moon.

If you deserved me then why did you hurt me?

It's not your soul, it's your ego that's worthy.

Here comes the sun.

Molt

Sun comes and bliss occurs,
The moon comes
And I'm lost for words;

The worms rise and here come the birds;

After crawling inside the skull of a decaying corpse
They've too embraced their fate –

Life is made of moments and
The memories that they make...

Pass Away

I'm excited to sleep
To get away from my mind,
A fear of heartache
And a prisoner to time –

If you'd let yourself be free
Then all will flow –

If you'd let me love you
Then we will always grow.

Here

Reality hit
And so did you –
All is different
And now we're through;

I go to sleep and wish to forget –
Only to wake up to a new day
Where we have not yet met –

The present is here,
Not over there –

I'm grateful for the memories
And the times that we shared.

A Pleading Letter

Why can't you just accept what I value
And love me through?
Why can't you kiss me till the sky turns blue?

Why is it that what you prefer is more important
Than what I prefer?
Why can't we both prefer together?

Why is my comfort such a problem for you?
Why must you project your challenging
Circumstances and jealousy upon me?
Why must you hurt me?
My comfort was once of your essence
Until it wasn't.

You used to admire my values and
Now it's a problem to the ego
But not to *you*!

Why can't we just be one happy family?
How can you say you don't care? –
About making love or even affection?
How could you say that *this* means
Nothing to you and does nothing for you? –

This means that no moment we shared was true
Because it was just acted upon to fulfill your
Fairytale ending –
You were only looking to get something out of it –

You were only looking to the future and
You were devaluing every moment of the Present
That you've experienced by lying to yourself.

But again,
I'm aware this isn't you –
The gracious love is in there locked away
But I can no longer wait,
I've had my stay –

Pray and wish for material gifts and
You'll be an endless prisoner;
Earn your place in life by
Embracing your highest duty –
This very moment
And it's innate beauty.

This may sound like berating
But this is from just a place of hurt –

I must now go to the soil
And bury myself in dirt –

The beginning is able to be eternal
If you separate yourself from the mind.

God created the mind out of Time
To teach a valuable lesson:
Timelessness.

Stream of Thought

Narcissus loves himself superficially –

All is external and the reflection is only
Temporal comfort –

What they see becomes what they want –
Their values are tied to an illusion –

The reflection is too murky to see the
Universal glimmer within his eyes –

When hope to the future becomes a prison
Rather than love of the eternal present
And what is
All life truly dies.

Storytelling

"I'm all alone – poor me," said the forever victim.

"Yes, I know," echoed the story.

Don't take this parable the wrong way
Because truthfully there is no right way.

Let this be soup for the buried soul –

Heal yourself from the story's hole.

Regardless of however true your myth,
What you tell yourself
Determines your bliss.

The Greatest Pain

There's a piece of me that wishes you still loved me.

I'm mixed up and confused and
I don't want to see you.

I want to run away and no longer be you.

My face holds back the tears and tension;
My jaw, the back of my head,
My face, my eyes;
Emotions manifest in parts of the body
As tightness and pain.

It's as if I'm attempting to hold onto you.

I must let you go.

It's time to let you go.

It looks like I had my own story too –

It looks like I'm bitter that it didn't work out.

I don't blame you nor do I name you.

I think the truth of the matter is that
We're so perfect together,

And I feel the unconditional love off of you
When you're not lost in your mind.

The problem is you're in your head most of the time.

The problem is you're part of the clock.

I tremble to the sound of your voice.

I'm scared to look you in the eye.

It all hurt so bad.

We can't do this anymore.

I didn't know how hard it would be
To think of you with someone else –

Now I have to see it –

In this moment I'm not mature enough –
In this moment I'm not at peace and
Hold the maturity to accept it –

I thought our bond was unbreakable –

Let me tell you what I do have:

The maturity to acknowledge that I think
All of these thoughts that stem from an
Uneasy feeling –

Stories are just stories –

Awareness is what it is.

I do have the wisdom to know that
I must go –

Unless the egoless you comes back.

Love yourself so we can love each other.

More

I sleep to get away from the pain,
To rest my body when I hear your name –

My face is tight like a drum
While I choke on my tears;

Once again,
I gave the power to someone to
Evoke my deepest fears –

But this doesn't mean that
I cannot make myself whole.

Somber slumber begins as I journey to put the
Pieces together in my mind –

With the poisonous hope to wake anew –

Wakeup from this walking sleep!

You are a man.

You are not a sheep.

Tick-tock

Memories of the past bleed into the present
To remind you that you're still alive...

The good and the bad –
It's what we choose to thrive.

I'm wasting my energy on you;
I'm wasting valuable moments of my life on you –
I'm wasting away.

Fiction

Every moment we shared was a lie
Because you were never truly there –
But I know you were.

There was always an end to meet your needs –
There was always a plan –
But you were present and beautiful.

You'll justify the voice in your head
Because that's all you choose to know –
But you're not the voice in your head.

The more challenging your story
The stronger your identification with it becomes –
But you can overcome it by truly accepting it.

I sought after nothing from you
Other than to share my unconditional love –
I wouldn't change a thing.

Now I want to hide from you and
I tremble at the sound of your voice –
But I still dream of our songs.

I'm hurt – I had a hope you'd return –
I still feel you inside of me.

I guess we were both hanging ourselves
From the poisonous rope of hope –
But there is truth in our love.

Once Upon A Time

There once was a time when we were so present with
one and other that nothing could shatter us –

This could've been eternal but stories and the chatter
Of the mind took away from the glimmer in the eye –

I still see it on occasion –
I still see the freedom –
I still feel the unconditional love.

If I could build you a house with no windows to look
Out of and mirrors of our eyes' reflections
Surrounding the inside then I would –

Maybe then you would realize that bliss is internal
Rather than external.

Then you couldn't get away from the truth –

Even upon shattering the mirrors the truth would be
Etched upon your soul.

No conditioned mind or thought can conceive this –
Look within.

Our love was pure. Our love is pure.

Simplicity

In the oceanic sky lights flash,
A hue from the universe consoles me
From the moon's cast.

Repeat

Driving by I slowly die
As love once ripped us apart –

Now I write to the midnight hue as
My heart beats to the dark –

I've made myself a stranger to you
Because my heart's in danger –

You see,
When a house is no longer a home
Then one's mind truly roams;
But not to be set wild and free,
It'd rather be tortured and drowned in the sea –

You couldn't just let us be...
I've seen it, I've felt it, it's unworldly!

You couldn't just let yourself be free!

Your story became you!

Over and over and over again
I mourn the death of my best friend –

You talk of "God" yet you show now awareness to
Our Creator's truest gift –

Smell the flowers,
Take a whiff –

I would never tell anyone how to live,
Or manipulate a mind to burn a bridge –

I write from truth that is not lead by egoic feeling –
I write to ground you and to promote a world
Filled with healing –

I saw into your soul and in those moments
You were whole – You Still are –

This is not some utopian illusion,
Nor is it lust or the mind's confusion,
Here and now, I write to tell you
That bliss isn't bought or taught –

You've talked yourself to believe that all is a lie
And in doing so you constantly die –

You believe your story and I can show you
That it's a lie –

All because I saw it in your eyes:
It was when you let yourself finally die.

The Story

"We could be so good together,"
The ego somberly cried
While the Present Self runs and hides –

A dream, an illusion, a mind filled with confusion,
And a burden so heavy that it's surely worth losing –

Moments and memories never die
But people surely do –
Sometimes even while they're still alive –

I can say I love you while
I wish to the stars above you –

I wear time on my heart and around my neck,
A broken clock to be exact,
To exemplify that being a prison to Time
Wastes nothing but Time –
Yet Time itself is an illusion.

Love is formless.

Drained

All out of tears,
All out of fears,
All out of time,
All out of wine –

The ego is so strong that it feels like it's real –

I cried myself to sleep just to let my ego die –
I spit it out in tears
And now salt
Still scars my eyes.

Tangled Web

What truly breaks my heart is knowing that you'll let
Them see the best of you,
Your charming most inner presence –

You'll capture them in the web
And attack them when your good and ready –

You'll lose your Higher Self as you devour their soul
To make you feel more whole –

It was all too real,
Too real for you –

Your dreams are based on others,
They are stories,
They aren't you –

You'll fight with my words but
If you were going to die tomorrow,
I know that you'd give me your heart –

Because you know that I love you,
And the moments we shared are above you –

Tears while I looked into your eyes –
Moments like that can never die –
And believe it or not they
Have no purpose or intention:
And that is how valuable they are.

Divine Intervention.

Now

Everything worked in the beginning
Because you let it –
And then difficulties came
And so did your story –

Nothing binds the heart other than the mind
And its planned intentions –

In the movie we would end up together,
In the book we would end up apart;

In my mindless mind we are forever,
In my heart we are the dark –
But in my soul we will never part.

Love

Love is a drug
That's stronger than reason –
Don't fall for it
Or you'll be accused
Of treason.

The Rain

Rain gently falls
Along with my thoughts,
Earth now speaks
As each drop
Connects the dots.

Prisoner

The addiction to conflict
And drama begins
In order to escape from the painful reality –

Everything becomes an obstacle,
Everyone becomes an enemy,
Every situation becomes a distraction –

The world is viewed as toxic as
One's own toxicity is projected –

The Higher Self lets in brief moments of bliss
In order to innately thrive,
Only to soon be tainted by
The constructed egoic story –

The forever prisoner –
The forever victim –

Where does it end? – simply where it begins.

The endless beginning –
Oh, how I love you.

Déjà Vu

The moment he realized
That he couldn't help her –

The moment that the present
Became the past –

The moment that the young boy
Pleaded to the woman to stop drowning herself,
He had realized that he could not save her –

She had to let herself drown
In order to see the light –
She had to save herself.

Attachment

The fixation was with your form
When I devalued our love –

It was when you became a stone that it became
Difficult for me to be soft and yielding
Because I wasn't *being* –

It is the formlessness that I love in you –
It is the energy that is invisible to the eye
Yet paradoxically lives within it and too beyond it
To realms unknown but most definitely felt –

In kind fact, it makes my heart melt.

Stars

Full moon,
I had seen it when I closed my eyes;

I grew fearful of the emptiness
And all subsided –

By the light of the moon
My spirit was guided.

Pain

This sadness is madness,
It doesn't truly exist!

There's this space between the breath
That we frequently tend to miss.

Sky

Fluffy white clouds,
Vast blue sky;

I look to you
And *I* finally dies.

Shakes

Withdrawing from your love
As I crave a present kiss,

All was so much beauty,
All was so much bliss –

And now this "Time" is missed.

Nature

If I could heal your soul
And take away your pain,

I would command a thunderstorm
To submerge it in the rain –

Feel it and embrace it;
Take on the darkness and taste it –

Don't become it because it isn't truly you;
Shine the light of Reason
And the clouds will part too.

Here

The green – the rain
The smell – the pain

All recedes into the silent forest
While gifted the melody
Of its gentle chorus;

No thing or thought
Can find me here –

Not even a story
Or my darkest fear –

I am home.

The Moon

Full moon,
I saw it when I closed my eyes;

I grew fearful and then let it subside –
The mind fears a deeper sense of presence
In which it cannot comprehend;

As soon as this is questioned
The experience then ends.

Feel

Feel, let go –

Love, just grow.

Intimate

Gentle kisses from the earth
As it again reminds me
Of my worth –

Rustling leaves in the cool wind
Give me hugs with no end –

Silence comes
While all who watch go to sleep –

We walk in pain
But we no longer weep.

Ego

The ego only listens
To what it wants to hear –

It clings to thought out of endless fear –

It masks itself as reality
And in the judgement of its peers.

Expect

Expectations and attachment
All just fades away –

They're delusions of the mind
And nothing that ever stays –

Trust in the space
Between the trees –
Trust in the love
Between your knees.

Eyes

We crossed paths and I couldn't yet laugh;

My stomach dropped to the sound of your voice –

Reminding me that within us
I never had a choice –

I peered into your eyes
And you were no longer there,

From that day on I lost my song
And my favorite tune –

She lost herself in Time and Greed
And forgot she's one with the moon,
So, I now bleed.

Trapped

A moth that's trapped between the veil of life
Attempts to be free –

I see myself within him and so
I set him on a tree.

Space

Give me space to find myself
As an object in time
Around nobody else.

Remember

A utopia lies in the future
But I exist right here;

Our presences is the value
That surpasses our deepest fears –

Truth then becomes youth
And Time becomes a noose –

Seeing through the stories
We begin to feel beyond time or reason –

We heal ourselves,
We love ourselves,
We grow with the seasons.

Possession

If you do not choose to step out of
I, me, my, or *you,*
The sky will stay black and
Never turn blue.

Stare

I'm split in two
While I look at you –

Sickened by
Your look,
Your smile,
Walking death,
Won't you stay awhile –

But then I realized I was too drowning in the sea,
I was attached to your misery and
I couldn't let it be –

I assure you that this isn't you;
When you realize this,
The sky will turn blue –

I remember. I remember.

Betrayal

I picture you
With another man,
I picture you
Walking hand in hand –

I picture you sharing kisses,
I picture us and our reminisces –

I picture you making love,
I picture you in new love –

My ego taunts me
And tells me that this is love,
But we all know that this isn't true
And that love is none of the above –

But here is what is true,
My attachment is not to you
But the presence that we shared,
It is within ourselves that we grew
Absent of Time and without care –

Now I write from attachment
While reflecting on an unearthly experience –

I am now letting go
Because the ego is projecting weariness.

Reflection

The times we could've had,
You threw everything away
That is meaningful to you
And you are so unconscious
That you believe that you are awake –

I accept it and I am moving on –

No more excuses –

No more mistakes –

I must be kind to myself
And eventually I will forgive you,
But right now, I feel hurt and betrayed
Because you threw your Higher Self away –

You are still not back –
This is your path –
This is not mine –

Our love is Divine and absent of Time.

Remember your eyes.

Remember your tears.

Remember your smile –
It erased the years.

Nothing

I fear nothing – I fear no thing.

My heart and soul
Are in the right place
But my mind can't stand
The sight of your face –

I is done –
I accept that this chapter has ended
And that *we* are through –

My skies may now be black,
But again, they'll soon turn blue –

What great pain –
Here comes the rain.

Remember

Everything was bliss until it wasn't –
Do you remember the moment that it changed? –

When you got lost in your thoughts
And become consciously insane? –

The toxic voices are always choices
And for the most part are always there –
They may be a part of us
But we don't need to care –

You're trapped in a story that is never-ending –
It's so strong that it's worth befriending –

I've given myself but now I must step back,
All you put forth are a series of traps –

I remember all of those genuine words
That I know your truly meant
But your Presence is lost
And now you choose to silently repent;

We could've been doing this,
We could've been doing that,
But instead, your ego turned
Into a blood-sucking bat –

We became lost when *I* was solidified –
We was never truly two but it was actually one –
This is when all was bliss –
This was when all was "fun" –
The beginning never ends.
The beginning never ends.

Past

You've said words that are beyond reason,
You attacked my values and
Waged war with the seasons –

I've been torturing myself for far too long,
I've been sitting here waiting to again hear your song,

But I was wrong –

So now I dream all nightmare long –

The ego disguised my innate sense of being
With its stories –
Upon writing this I've again
Found my unshakable glory.

Accept

I'm ready to forgive you, I will –

Until the acceptance,
My heart will till and turn over soil
Until a new seed is sewed
And a new path is paved on this endless road –

Let the rain come
And let kindness heal –

I attempts to protect itself
From what is far too real –

I is addicted to chaos but 'I' am not I –
Once you realize this
You will peacefully die –

If you continue to plant seeds of doubt
You'll forever decay –

The more you water the soil,
The more you lose your way.

Home

When a house is no longer a home,
Dead memories haunt the halls –

Solitude only exists outside amidst the clouds –

A home decays – it screams so loud –

The flame withers as it chooses to no longer breathe.

I have let you kill me for the last time –

Because how can you destroy space that is
Invisible and only felt –

I was holding on for far too long,
As I sing my song –

Just as a melody is Nature's greatest presence,
The creation is that much more –

Adding harmony to life opens the endless door.

Letter

You broke my heart
And tore us apart
But I truly do not blame you –

I hold bitterness and hate
But this shall not seal our fate
As space begins to save you.

Robins

Hungry baby birds
I'm lost for words –

Yellow butterfly along with pollinating bees,
Beautiful laughter and the tall green trees –

There is nothing else.

There is *nothing* else...

Time

And in the end, he had lost her to Time,
The egoic fire had consumed her mind –

The delusion finally became her reality
That she continued to live in,
A dream that was never truly hers –

She tossed aside her purpose
And threw away her song –

She lost herself to form
Despite her God never being "wrong."

Film

If life was a movie,
There would be a happy ending –
But I ask you:
Does this feel happy?
Is this even an ending?
Do you fear the happy ending? –
Because you fear your great Presence?

Emotions are temporal,
The acceptance of the present moment
And what calls you to it
Brings upon bliss that is not of this world –

If there is only a beginning –
There is no end.

Where?

Where did I go? –
My mind briefly went crazy,
I felt lost in myself and like
No one could save me –

I observed and watched the rush of thoughts
That were stemming from the ego's emotions
Along with its greatest plots –
It was a passing storm,
A moving train,
Because I remained present,
Because I remained sane –

Tears were soon to follow
As I was too sick to wallow –
I was done with this unkind state
But patience was needed
And not impatient hate –
I put kindness forth
And I there I went –

And then there you were
In that very moment –
Tears again fell from my eyes
As I consoled a little angel –
I waved goodbye
And again, I cried –

My mind then started to wander
To the day we died –
And then I looked to the sky
And all subsided –
We were no longer apart,
We were no longer divided.

The Beginning

Oh, how your words echo in my mind,
The pain and confusion,
The elaborate kind;

Masked by the ego
And disguised with guilt,
Followed by acidic tears
That will soon to wilt
The flower of our love
That once vibrantly bloomed –

Now I write to no one
And I follow the moon.

Where did you go?

Tall

Walking amidst the tall green trees
My mind wanders to endless seas –

I wanted to save her but I couldn't,
I wanted to save her but I couldn't –

I had to let her drown
Because she was pulling me under,
For suffering is all she chose to know –

She is governed by thoughts
And believes she is her mind,
She is completely lost
And a prisoner to Time –

But I once saw the light within her eyes
That was beyond reason,
Salvation will come and
Too follow the seasons.

Family

A family doesn't push each other away,
A family is grateful, not hateful,
And forever stays –

A family is not a family
When you push everyone away,
A family's not a family when
One can no longer stay –

A friend's no longer a friend
When you are no longer there –
A love is no longer a love
When time interferes –
A love is no longer a love
As soon as the ego reappears –

Don't stay trapped inside,
Don't be a prisoner to the judgement of others,
Love yourself,
Don't let our flame smother –
The light is you,
I just shared the key –
It is truly our love
That set you forever free –

This is deeper than the mind
And I saw it in your eyes –
None of this is you,
Despite the fact that you seemingly died.

Kind

I again get lost
In the kindness of my heart,
I must separate the light
Before it too becomes dark –

If it's creating misery,
It's not the gentle way;
If it's creating sorrow,
Then do not let it stay –

Mind yourself when the misery
Is your doing –
Food for thought,
This is surely worth chewing –

I again and again find myself
Through the words that I do not own –
I write to the hungry birds
And again, find my home.

Storm

Torrential rain,
Please wash away my old pain
While I sit here on the floor,

As I sit, I feel your lips,
As my skin dances to each drip
And *needs* no more.

Free

The stars are so vibrant –

You've been gone for so long
That I'm afraid you're not coming back –

Your pain body is too strong
And wants to live on.

Poem

A poem a day is a moment
In time that leads to now –

I was holding onto your love
And the presence that we vowed –

But through my journaled words
I can see our demise –

The problem is
I don't see it in your eyes –

The attachment to Time is truly living death
Except without peace –

If you want to know how much I love you,
Let your soul read my words
And not your mind –

They are absent of the ego
And devoid of any time –

If you want to find your present self,
Read my words,
If you want to find our love,
Read my words,

If your mind tries to argue with them
Then they are no longer our words.

Punish

You've been pushing me away
And I can no longer stay,
This pain has had my attention
And it cannot live another day –

You unknowingly punish me
Because your ego didn't get
What it wanted –

So now, you scream and are taunted;

It's you that pushed me away,
It's you that could no longer stay –

You fear happiness,
You hate yourself,
And you push away anything
That truly heals your soul –

I wish and pray that you again find peace
While I tear and gaze to the swaying trees –

You used to tell me that you loved my mind
But that's not what you loved –
You loved my presence
Because it is a doorway to your own –

It is the kingdom within.

I now look to the memories up in the sky
Where they endlessly run and never die –
Like our untainted love.

Cry

I'm tired of crying,
I'm tired of dying –

When will I be all out of tears?

When will time stop and heal all of my fears?

When will I accept the loss of my love?

If this is that easy for you to move on then
Our love wasn't true –

If our presence was this easy to erase
Then it's you that I will not face too –

It may have been hiding for far too long
But it never will die
Because it is our song.

Midnight

Guided by the moon
But clouded with your beauty –

The addiction to drama
And the need for more –

Take a breath
And open the door.

The Star

I saw a falling star
And was about to make a wish,

I instead breathed in all of its beauty
And was transported then to bliss.

The Breath

I breathe and truly feel;

Tears then begin to heal.

Music

The music is calling and
My heart is falling –

How many times must I tell myself
That "it's okay"? –

I whisper to the sky as
Stars fall away –

Guide me, love –

Where shall I go?

Time will tell
And no one knows.

The Ego

My ego is fixated on you
But my presence feels something higher,

When I mix the two
My mind goes on fire –

If I'm to lose you
I will survive –

But there's something more,
We are meant to thrive –

Tall still trees and vibrant seas.

The Thought

I thought about you
And laughed in glee –

There is no you
Nor is there me.

Lust

I look at your lips
And long for them –

They were made for mind –

If you want to know how much I love you
Then look deep within yourself –

If you want to know how much I love you
Then don't seek it in anybody but yourself.

The Addict

I was addicted to love –

I had withdrawals –

I craved your absolute presence –

I became too attached to the
Essence of who you are –

I became attached to the forever moment –

I became lost in myself by becoming lost in you
When you lost yourself –

I craved the presence of you
While neglecting my own,
Our own –

I neglected life by separating my oneness from it.

Wanderer

I spend most of my day
Lost in thought
While I find myself in the sky –

While I find myself in the trees –

I am lost –

I do not know what I want –

I want nothing –

I want no thing –

I has died.

Sick

I'm tired of the story,
I'm tired of the attachment, resistance, insecurities,
All that are holding me from my glory –

Let things go!

Let things die!

What is invisible to the eye is essential –
What isn't is consequential –

Once again you held back out of fear,

Time fades away in your eyes
As you look for more reasons to hide –

I've made up stories and was completely wrong;
I cried, I died, I said my song –

Fuck it, *who* cares –

It's time to live on.

Babies

Little bird beaks,
They barely speak but make my mind weak
And lost for words –

Their presence is felt,
It makes my heart melt,

It seems that I'm too one with the birds.

Moment

Enjoy the moment,
What will be will be;

Just forgive yourself
And you'll be free –

The sky is on fire
As my heart withers in desire –

Where did I go?

What do I know?

Dad

The moons reflection soothes the soul;
My father and I sing
While being whole –

The deep presence
Resides in the forest sky;

The deep breaths of presence
That never truly dies.

Deceive

The beauty is that there is no beauty –

The beauty is the moments that fool me –

The beauty is that there is no thing more –

The beauty is opening the door.

Hiding

The moon hides behind
The silhouette of vine covered trees –

While two lost souls
Just simply must be.

Movement

What moves first? –
The heart or the clock?

What moves second? –
The light or the dark?

As bliss fills me
Nothing kills me –

I'm light as a feather,
I'm one with the weather –

I'm here and nowhere,
I'm lost without a care –

If you can hear me,
I love you –

If you can hear me,
Dreams come true.

Pain

Heavy eyes,
I lay in bed;

I take a breath
And rest my head –

We are the light of love;
Nothing below,
Nothing above.

Closer

Get close and let me breathe you in,
Give me your hand
And we'll be whole again –

The look in your eyes
Attempts to break away –

I breathe in your heart
And
In it I stay –

Guide me,
Show me which way to go –

Listen and feel the space between your breath
And
In this *you* will grow.

Cardinal

You are one of the most beautiful creatures
That I've ever had the privilege to lay eyes on –

In all respect,
There's something that calls me to you;
It may be the pain within your eyes –

In this moment,
My soul wants to dance with yours;
Desires set your soul on fire –

As I close my eyes
I feel your touch
In the wind of the dusky silhouetted trees
That hug my vibrating soul –
I am whole.

Speak

Tell me you love me,
I long for you
As I rewind your blossoming smile –

Precious lily, won't you stay awhile?

If it all ends, will it all begin?

Can I hold your hand? –
Can we dance again?

I smell you as you bloom
While we dance to the wind and moon.

Creator

Look what God created,
How divine –

I sit here, still –
I smile at my thoughts –

I dance in the kitchen
While breathing in the vegetable gravy –

There is nothing to do –
There is no one to save me –

The sky grounds me
While love surrounds me:
Nothing else –

The sky and its beauty;
The artist and his duty.

Speak

All is still,
It's time that kills –

When you fade away
And no longer pray
You will have survived another day.

Chair

I sit,
I think,
I laugh –

I feel and see it all –
'I' is absent;
I have become nothing –

I am one with all –
I no longer know my thoughts –

The silhouette of dancing trees
Are etched upon my eyelids,
Just as my unintentioned intentions
Move my pen to guide this:

Up

Open sky,
Candy clouds;

I care about nothing
And this screams so loud –

Calm like a blade of grass;
Calm like memories that last –

Empty, no words –
All is simple as the sky –

The ocean calls
And then we die.

Invisible

The way you look,
The way you smell,
The way you taste,
The way you tell –

I don't know what it is
But I'm drawn to your light
When you are home –
I love you madly;
I love all but I love you and the role you play –

I've tamed you,
Can't you see?

I don't own you
Nor do you own me
But our "need" for each other is
Beyond what is essential and
Beyond flesh and blood –
One might say it's too even found
In the mind.

Love

True love knows no time,
True love knows no age,
True love knows nothing,
True love accepts all,
True love seeks nothing,
True love wants nothing,
True love needs nothing –

True love is absent of the mind,
True love is devoid of time,

True love is letting go
When the Seed of Presence
No longer shows.

Mirror

Look at all of the emotions that arise
When you think of our demise –

Look at the possession you seek
That is making you weak –

Contemplate our memories
Before they were intentions,

Contemplate your words
And their deepest reflections –

Contemplate the love for me
That lingers deep beyond your mind,

Contemplate the separation
Between age and time,

Contemplate the blissful presence
That we once shared,

Contemplate the beginning
When all we had was care;

Now, look into my eyes
And tell me that I'm not the love of your life,

If you think this is true
Then your mind has become a knife –

Contemplate why "I'm different,"
This is simply because I am
The purest *you* –

Despite the tears that I've wept
I assure you we are not through –

The beginning can be the endless beginning
If our minds don't let it end,

If we feel beyond intentions
Present souls will too soon mend –

I am life itself and so are you:
The midnight sky,
The sunset's hue.

I'll Show You

You asked me how I could even love you,
And I told you because *you* is not truly you;

We shared what was not of this world
Until it was locked away
And all was seemingly through,

As the ego grew that still wasn't you
Presence seemed to no longer stay,
The blissful children
Then no longer played –

"I've never felt like this before,"
Because "this" is not a feeling
Nor can it be *felt*;
This is the greatest gift of all,
This presence
Is the soul that melts –

When Time became the answer
It soon became a cancer –

What you did and what you said
And how you misinterpreted my deeply felt words,
Have painted a picture of great pain
That made the mind's story absurd and insane,
And now I write to the hungry birds –

Crossing paths as you go on to give
The temporal presence that I love,
My heart breaks while I re-contemplate
All of the above –

We birthed beauty into this world

And you attempt to devalue its meaning,
It is not even truly of this world
And this is what sent you gleaming
Into here and now,
Into even God's breath
I solemnly vow –

It's as if I seek to put together words
To heal your tarnished soul
But I already know
That within your present essence
You are already whole –

I play and sing for myself
With the wish that you would hear,
To again find your Presence
And to release all of your ego's fears –

He'll see the best of you
And this is what kills me;
He'll see the life in you,
The same life that thrilled me –

Remember that I never wanted
Or needed anything from you,
And I remember for you it was the same;
Remember when there was innate love
And not a desired gain –

Remember when there was no future,
Nor was there a past –
Remember when it was the beginning,
Remember when it didn't last:
The moment that Time interfered,
The moment that Presence disappeared –

The moment that the ego reappeared.

One might ask: What does this do for *me?*
And I'll tell you again that "this" isn't *you.*

Once you realize this power,
The skies will again turn blue.

A utopia is in the future and
If you want a glimpse into the future
Then look deep within my eyes to the Present,
The Universe's greatest gift
That no wealth could ever buy;
Embrace it now
And don't ask how,
Just breathe and all subsides –

The breath is a reflection of
Its ever-healing selfless self,
Formless and empowering
That gives life to everything else.

The kingdom of heaven lies within,
It sits in the eyes of your best friend,
It is not over there or somewhere else,
It is Here right now,
Even when by yourself;
It lives within
Through thick and thin –

The mind cannot truly conceptualize
The Divine Energy of God
In which I speak,
I've dug much deeper
And sometimes I go weak,
But I assure you that through the

Love of the egoless Self,
You will naturally embrace everyone else –

Allow it to be the endless beginning,
You will never cheat yourself,
You will always be winning.

Thought is superficial when it stems from egoic fears,
The mind then becomes a prison
That leaves one in endless tears –

If you desire to argue against these deeply felt words
Then ask yourself who's speaking or judging,
Ask yourself what it's worth –
And if it's worth something
Then it's worth nothing.

The Mirror of Presence

There we were,
Sitting together as if nothing had happened;
Smiling, laughing – utterly present...
Is this not true love?

This peace is felt as soon as nothing
Is wanted or needed –

Despite your absolute beauty of form,
What drew me into you,
What draws me into you
Is beyond the depths of your ocean-blue eyes –

For quite sometime I had lost myself
But then found it again in your eyes –

You didn't complete me
Nor did we complete each other –

We were one – we are one –

You were right,
The words "I love you," are not enough –

But this unintentional feeling surely is –

It's not of reality yet oddly it is one with it –

It's not even a feeling because it's beyond emotions
And one with the ocean –

Do you "feel" *it?* –
If you can then that's not *it* –
Because it is not a choice nor a voice –

It is beyond thought and is oneness –

"Essentiel est invisible à l'œil nu"

True love conquers all
Because it is one with all
In the moment that is begins
And never ends.

As the stare weakens and turns to a gaze,
The doorway to presence is embraced,
And the Light of Peace becomes one's taste –

If you're reading this, just know that
I love you –

If you're reading this, just know that
I am you.

Presence & Its Shadow

Here I am at peace
While old chatter appears
Within the confines of my ears –

Birds chirp,
The cool breeze,
The sun's tickle,
A vibrant sneeze –

The humming of the Universe
And its melodic song
To remind "me" of my worth
Beyond *right* or *wrong* –

An angel's voice
And a shadow behind it;
These precious memories
And the way we define it –

The rooted tree sculpted
Amidst the spacious sky;
The forever poem
That never dies –

Just as the dark defines the light
And
The night defines the day,

The shadow defines Presence
And
The breath defines the way...

Presence &
Its Shadow